So Cute! Baby Animals

Calves

By Julia Jaske

Baby cows like to moo.

Baby cows like to eat.

Baby cows like to sit.

Baby cows like to explore.

Baby cows like to chew.

Baby cows like to herd.

Baby cows like to run.

Baby cows like to jump.

Baby cows like to lick.

Baby cows like to stand.

Baby cows like to hug.

Baby cows like to sleep.

Word List

Baby	explore	lick
cows	chew	stand
moo	herd	hug
eat	run	sleep
sit	jump	

60 Words

Baby cows like to moo.
Baby cows like to eat.
Baby cows like to sit.
Baby cows like to explore.
Baby cows like to chew.
Baby cows like to herd.
Baby cows like to run.
Baby cows like to jump.
Baby cows like to lick.
Baby cows like to stand.
Baby cows like to hug.
Baby cows like to sleep.

Published in the United States of America by Cherry Lake Publishing Group
Ann Arbor, Michigan
www.cherrylakepublishing.com

Book Designer: Melinda Millward

Photo Credits: © EASY PHOTO/Shutterstock, cover, 1; © Sophia Floerchinger/Shutterstock, 2; © Andrés Cuenca/Shutterstock, 3; © Cornel Constantin/Shutterstock, 4; © Lukas Guertler/Shutterstock, 5; © Oaisu/Shutterstock, 6; © Pawel Papis/Shutterstock, 7; © Jackson Stock Photography/Shutterstock, 8; © carlprescott_photo/Shutterstock, 9; © Brian Dunne/Shutterstock, 10; © Clara Bastian/Shutterstock, 11; © Jeffrey Schwartz/Shutterstock, 12; © Adam Middleton/Shutterstock, 13; © Eric Isselee/Shutterstock, 14

Copyright © 2023 by Cherry Lake Publishing Group
All rights reserved. No part of this book may be reproduced or utilized in any form or by any means without written permission from the publisher.

Cherry Blossom Press is an imprint of Cherry Lake Publishing Group.

Library of Congress Cataloging-in-Publication Data

Names: Jaske, Julia, author.
Title: Calves / written by Julia Jaske.
Description: Ann Arbor, Michigan : Cherry Lake Publishing, [2022] | Series: So cute! Baby animals
Identifiers: LCCN 2022009913 | ISBN 9781668908808 (paperback) | ISBN 9781668911990 (ebook) | ISBN 9781668913581 (pdf)
Subjects: LCSH: Calves—Juvenile literature.
Classification: LCC SF205 .J37 2022 | DDC 636.2/07—dc23/eng/20220330
LC record available at https://lccn.loc.gov/2022009913

Cherry Lake Publishing Group would like to acknowledge the work of the Partnership for 21st Century Learning, a Network of Battelle for Kids. Please visit http://www.battelleforkids.org/networks/p21 for more information.

Printed in the United States of America
Corporate Graphics